DEAR DAVID

H. S. Vigeveno

G/L
REGAL
BOOKS
™

A Division of G/L Publications
Glendale, California, U.S.A.

Other good Regal reading by H.S. Vigeveno:
Climbing Up the Mountain
Is It Real?
Jesus the Revolutionary
The Listener
13 Men Who Changed the World
I Know How It Feels

Scripture quotations, unless otherwise indicated,
are from the *New American Standard Bible.* © The
Lockman Foundation 1960, 1962, 1963, 1968, 1971.
Used by permission.
Other versions used are:
KJV The Authorized King James Version.
NEB *The New English Bible.* © The Delegates
of the Oxford University Press and The Syndics
of the Cambridge University Press 1961, 1970.
Reprinted by permission.
Phillips Letters to Young Churches,
J.B. Phillips, Translator. © 1947 by
The Macmillan Company.

Published by Regal Books Division, G/L Publications
Glendale, California 91209
Printed in U.S.A.

Library of Congress Catalog Card No. 77-86534
ISBN 0-8307-0594-5

introduction

This is an intimate and very personal document. I have shared my innermost thoughts and feelings following the sudden, shocking death of my only son.

It has been painful to do so, but it has also been therapeutic.

The one and only reason why I am willing to bare my soul lies in my earnest desire to help someone else who is struggling with grief and loss. If my honesty strikes a responsive chord, if fear and guilt and doubt can be overcome, and if God uses these words to create hope where grief runs rampant, the recording of my sorrow will not have been in vain.

My sighing is all my food,
and groans pour from me in a torrent.
Every terror that haunted me
has caught up with me,
and all that I feared has come upon me.
There is no peace of mind nor quiet for me;
I chafe in torment and have no rest.

But I will not hold my peace;
I will speak out in the distress of my mind
and complain in the bitterness of my soul.
(Job 3:24–26; 7:11, NEB)

one

The last time I saw you, you were wearing your red T-shirt, blue denim pants, comfortable soft shoes and your contagious smile. You stepped into the station wagon with a fellow who was rapidly becoming one of your good friends. You were on your way to see his sister who had a typical teenager's crush on you. You were going places, and your friend allowed you to drive that wagon!

I didn't like that a bit; after all, you didn't have a license yet. But your friend assured me that you drove very well, and you were so proud turning down the street, showing me that you could handle the big car.

That was the last time I saw you. Little did we both dream that that very night your short but beautiful life would be stopped by a bullet fired by a very sick man.

You couldn't have known that the man who brandished a gun in front of you all evening long was unable to part with it. Without that gun he felt like nothing. With it he was a big shot. That weapon was his only power and authority, but how could you know he

5

would shoot you if you merely asked to see it? His mind recoiled just because you reached out for his gun, and in one split second he fired and took you from us. Just like that. He had no right to, but he did it. You never touched the weapon. But now we're left alone, without you, thinking about you, remembering.

And what memories! Do you have any idea how many memories flood our minds? You gave us so much, David, because you gave us yourself. Sure, you made life difficult at times, sometimes very difficult, but you also provided many good times. You were very special. I want you to know that. You were, and are, very special. I only hope that I communicated that to you while you were still here with us. I wanted so very much to let you know that. Always. I'm sure you knew it and felt it, and I hope you realize it even now.

I wish I could see you again, but that's impossible! Just another chance to see you, to touch you, to laugh with you, but it won't be. It can't be. It will never be. Death is so final. So completely final. And it all happened in such a split second—his finger pulled the trigger and the bullet sped for your young body.

They tell me that your last words were: "I'm shot," and you went down. You looked at your sister and added, "Sharon, I love you." You never opened your eyes again. I'm glad of that. The bullet hit a vital artery and you were gone in seconds. By the time the paramedics arrived, less than 15 minutes later, your heartbeat didn't register even a flutter. The EKG was absolutely flat. Of course they tried to revive you, but it was useless.

That was just as well, David. You were such a sensitive boy. You couldn't have taken it, lying there

6

helpless, unable to tell us all good-bye for the last time, unable to express your concern for us. We couldn't have come to you in time either, since you were wounded in your friend's house a half hour away from ours.

I'm glad you went quickly. It was merciful of God to allow you to go without suffering. But even as I reflect on God's mercy in this instance, I have other thoughts concerning justice and fairness. They bother me. I want to tell you about them, too.

I am sickened of life;
I will give free rein to my griefs,
I will speak out in bitterness of soul.
I will say to God, "Do not condemn me."
(Job 10:1,2, NEB)

two

So many Christian friends have assured us that you are with God. And I believe that. You are at peace. You are better off. You do not have to live in this wicked world. You were sometimes overwhelmed by those big talkers, mainly because you trusted people. You easily could have been pulled into trouble. Now you do not have to endure life's trials.

But let me be honest. Of course I am comforted to know you are with the Lord. However, believing and knowing that doesn't remove the pain and the hurt I feel. We have a great faith in the risen Jesus who has conquered death. He has promised to give us eternal life and His promise is sure. I believe that to be absent from the body is to be present with the Lord, even as the Bible teaches. But, as I said, there's an awful pain and loss for us who are left on the earth.

You were so full of life. You enjoyed living. I've hardly ever known anyone who was able to get so much in so short a time. You were always on the go. Even when you were sick you wanted to have a good time recuperating.

you did more things and saw more things and experienced more things in your less than 16 years than some people do in 40. And you were always eager for more.

That man had no right to fire at you! He had no right to take your life, to snuff it out as if it was of no consequence, to treat you as I would slap a mosquito when it lands on my arm.

That's one reason why it hurts so much to lose you. Yes, I know all the answers—you are with God, heaven has gained you, you are happy. Some people have written that you must be very busy working for the Lord. But you know what it's like for me? It's like a big, gaping cavity right in the middle of my chest, an emotional cavity. No one could live with anything like that physically; and I can barely survive it emotionally. That abyss is not being filled. Nothing will fill it. Your life has ended on earth. The twenty-second of July will always be a black day on my calendar.

I can't help it. In spite of all my faith I have that vapid emptiness. And for the moment all I can say is that only your presence can fill it. Only if you come bouncing in through the door again with all your boyish enthusiasm. But that isn't about to happen. Not ever again. And the truth of that is sometimes *more than* painful.

Save me, O God;
for the waters are come in unto my soul.
I sink in deep mire, where there is no standing:
I am come into deep waters,
where the floods overflow me.

Deliver me out of the mire, and let me not sink.
. . . .
Let not the waterflood overflow me,
neither let the deep swallow me up, . . .
Hear me, O Lord;
for thy loving-kindness is good:
turn unto me
according to the multitude of thy tender mercies.
And hide not thy face from thy servant;
for I am in trouble: hear me speedily.
(Ps. 69:1,2,14-17, KJV)

I'm sorry but I just have to tell you this honestly—my emotions are sometimes overwhelming. They roll over me like waves of the sea, and they do not stop. There is no way to stop them. It is so hard to put this into words. My feelings run so deep that exposing them to words seem to cheapen them, like merchandise marked down for a sale.

And those feelings are persistent. "I'll never see him again . . . I'll never see him again . . . I'll never see him again," repeats like the tick of the clock. Never stopping. Even though I believe in life eternal, believe in the certainty of the resurrection, the immediate sensation of shock and loss ingrains itself as if it is here to stay. Permanently. That's the way it's going to be. I may as well get used to it.

There's no relief from that. No relief at all. No one is able to give me that relief. Some sit with me in silence and understand. Some quietly express their love. Some help me look up. Yet no one bears the pain for me. No

13

one is there to relieve the inner torture, the overwhelming hurt, the gnawing emptiness that will never again be filled. *Never again* be filled by anyone!

I've lost the one person I had set my hopes on the most. I cared so much because there was something in you that kept on precipitating that love. You were like Abraham's Isaac, David's Absalom. What sorrow is like unto that sorrow? In my grief I hear David's fatherly heart lament over his rebellious but brilliant son: *O my son Absalom, my son, my son Absalom! Would I had died instead of you, O Absalom, my son, my son!* (2 Sam. 18:33).

The manner of your death at first was shrouded in mystery. We were told lies. The man who became an accomplice to the murder forced (through fear) four young people to lie to the police. And those lies were trumpeted far and wide before the whole pack broke open. The detectives were originally convinced that you had shot yourself accidentally, as the young people testified. But when the truth came out the police realized that you never touched the gun.

Your death could not be covered over with lies. That would have been a great injustice. You were shot and killed, and you did not provoke the murder! Now we will face a jury trial in Superior Court and relive the events over again.

Although it was hard sitting through that preliminary hearing, we were proud of your little sister. She testified so clearly and confidently to what she had seen. She was with you the moment the shot was fired. You would have been proud of her too, of the way she answered all the rapid questions of the brilliant defense attorney. He was impressed by your 14-year-old sister, for she told

14

the truth without getting tripped up by his crafty questions.

Your murderer pleaded guilty to involuntary manslaughter.

We all love you, David. We are all grieved. And we want justice to be done on your behalf. But, even so, we know justice will never bring you back. And that is the wound that will not yet heal.

Even if it should heal in years to come—although I don't think it will ever completely heal—do you think for a moment that we could forget you?

The Lord detests traitors and men of blood. . . .
Bring ruin on them, O God;
let them fall by their own devices. . . .
But let all who take refuge in thee rejoice,
let them for ever break into shouts of joy;
shelter those who love thy name,
that they may exult in thee.
(Ps. 5:6,10,11, NEB)

four

We had so many good times together. You gave me so much of yourself. I remember.

I think back to the hours we romped on the floor in the living room. Sometimes I'd let you ride on my back and we'd go around the house—I, on all fours, and you riding proud, wanting everyone else to notice you. We would wrestle together and then spread out on the floor to play family games. We never sat at tables.

Remember the hours we worked together solving math problems, learning to write and read? Hours. Sometimes you had difficulties, but we kept working at it, and you wanted to learn. You were always very inquisitive, and you mastered the basics. And then all of a sudden you took off, took off in the world of electronics, began investigating, working on projects, doing terrific things. We were all so encouraged by your gifts. You weren't long into your teens until you were fixing all kinds of electronic problems and working on television sets—your first love—tearing them inside and out and tracking down whatever problems lurked in their resistors and capacitors.

In earlier years we spent hours kicking and throwing balls in the backyard. But you were not overly interested in sports and you gravitated more and more toward electronics. I stood back and marveled when you bought intricate equipment like your color bar generator and your post marker sweep generator, and read pages and pages of instructions as you put them together. When you walked into a parts store or television repair place, the experts listened to you in amazement. They could tell you knew what you were talking about.

He had no right to take you from us! You had a good mind and a brilliant future. And you wanted so much to live. So very much. Why did he have to point that stupid gun at you for no reason and snuff out your active life in one split second? Where is there justice in that?

I remember how excited you were just a few weeks ago when we sat down with the representative from a correspondence school and you enlisted in a television course. You wanted to take those lessons, get your diploma and apply for work. All you got to finish was one lesson. You never started the second one.

Yes, I know, vengeance belongs to the Lord. It is not in our hands. But there must be justice. I want the courts to see to it that justice is done. But that gaping cavity will remain. There is no way that you will come bounding back again, place your arm around my shoulders and ask: "Are you OK, Dad?"

Can anything separate us from the love of Christ?

I have become absolutely convinced that
neither Death nor Life,
neither messenger of heaven
nor monarch of earth,
neither what happens today
nor what may happen tomorrow,
neither a power from on high
nor a power from below,
nor anything else in God's whole world
has any power to separate us from
the love of God in Jesus Christ our Lord!
(Rom. 8:35,38,39, Phillips)

five

Perhaps the Lord told you something about your funeral. I don't know. But you would have been happy with your friends. All of them. So many called; the phone rang all the while. They took it hard. Fellows and girls. The girls were usually in tears. They couldn't believe it. But they could tell I was not kidding when I told them what happened. Quite a few of the kids attended your funeral.

We chose six of your friends to be pallbearers, and you know what? Your girlfriend suggested that they wear what you wore the night you were killed. The fellows went out and bought themselves bright red shirts and blue denim pants and the same kind of soft shoes you wore. When I explained at the funeral, why they were dressed like that, you could see soft smiles and some tears welling up in a few eyes.

Have you heard that I arose to say a few words after the pastors spoke? You know why I did that? Because I believed you'd want me to. I remember when I used to preach and you sat in the pew looking up at me. You were always intent. You really tried to listen, and you understood most of what I was saying even when you were young. True, you haven't attended church for about a year, but I know you believed. You really did believe in Jesus. And we always prayed together at mealtimes and sometimes read a little from the Bible.

Anyway, I spoke at the funeral because I had an inner conviction that you would want me to! That feeling possessed me the first night you were taken away from us. So many people were helped as I shared because you spoke to them also! They've written about that service and it was touching to read their messages. Because I could believe, they believed. They came to comfort us but they went away comforted.

I thought you'd like to know that.

And gifts have come pouring in which we're giving to a memorial fund in your name. We're contributing a sound system for the new high school camp to be built at Forest Home Christian Conference Grounds. You remember Forest Home. We were there many times. Some years ago we dedicated a tree in your name. You always wanted to see it. Now your name will also be on the sound booth!

David, it's really lonely without you. You're so terribly missed. Not that you can help it. It's not your fault. I certainly wouldn't want you to feel badly. I guess loneliness and grief are just things we humans have to live with. When you love so much, it hurts so grievously.

But I'm convinced that it is better to love than to shut ourselves off in isolation. One thing you've done for me in this short period after your death is to make me want to love even more than I ever have. To really love and care, and not to hide my feelings.

The sorrows of death compassed me,
and the pains of hell gat hold upon me:
I found trouble and sorrow.
Then called I upon the name of the Lord;
O Lord, I beseech thee, deliver my soul.
Gracious is the Lord, and righteous;
yea, our God is merciful.

I love the Lord, because he hath heard
my voice and my supplications.
Because he hath inclined his ear unto me,
therefore will I call upon him
as long as I live.

Precious in the sight of the Lord
is the death of his saints.
(Ps. 116:3–5,1,2,15, KJV)

six

Your mother is doing very well. She has such a strong and vital faith. She believes in the Lord completely. She speaks often of heaven. She is confident that you are at peace, and I'm very glad about that.

Once in a while I catch the tears in her eyes. It's mostly when she talks about things you liked to do or said or when something reminds her about the past. I suppose that will always be. I don't really believe she will ever get over it, although the pain will lessen with the passing of the years.

With me it's a little different, David. Everyone says that I'm so strong, that I believe so much and that my faith strengthens their faith. I don't know how that can be when I hurt so deeply. I do believe. Yes, there is no question in my mind about God. I'm not asking "Why?" Sometimes I do, but it's not a very pressing thought. It's like an extra in a movie—he appears on the screen for a second and the camera moves away from him again. I'm not asking "Why?" because I know it isn't very healing.

Let me tell you how I feel. It's like that abyss I was

talking about in the middle of my inner being—the realization that you're never coming back, that you've gone forever. But it's even more than that: I won't have another chance to say anything to you, to share anything with you, to watch you grow, to see you enjoy life and live to the full as only you were able to do.

It's the devastating agony of unfairness, of injustice, of cruelty in the world. And suddenly I feel akin to all the other hurting humans who have experienced the cruelties and injustices of life. I can sense where they are, how they must feel. And that's terrible too—to realize there is such a company of suffering humanity. Why? What have we all done?

Nothing! Nor am I feeling guilty for what I may have done. I'm not interpreting *your* murder as a punishment for *my* sins. I'm beyond that. I don't believe for a moment that a loving God operates the world in such a manner. He would be far from loving if He demanded your life to get back at me. Whenever guilt rears its ugly head, I deal with it *as guilt.* And the mercy of God through the cross of Jesus is sufficient. I am forgiven. I go on. There is no relation between any guilt feelings and your death.

But the unfairness of it all! Why should you be struck down so suddenly, so completely? What did you do? You didn't deserve that treatment for your "sins." No, there is no relation between your sins and your being killed. The truth of it is that you were an innocent victim. You did not provoke, nor did you deserve that bullet in your chest.

And that is what is so hard for me! Do you understand? Not just because I hurt, or because I'm left alone nor that you won't be here anymore with us. But because you were struck down and your life was snatched from you, and you were not given a chance, and you became an innocent victim. It is for you that I hurt, for you that I feel this destructive emptiness.

There is no way to tell you that. No way to communicate the compassion I feel, no way to comfort you now, no way to let you know that you are very much loved. That sick man did you the harshest, worst injustice that any person could commit.

You were always so sensitive, David, so quickly hurt when people hurt you. Remember the night that punk busted into your room with a knife and stomped all over you? And we didn't even know about it until afterwards because your room was behind the garage with a separate entrance. How I hurt for you then. You sensed my anguish. You were lucky to get off with a few scratches and bruises (and a wounded spirit). But no broken bones or anything more serious.

Well, my anguish then was only a smidgen compared to what I'm feeling now. In spite of my solid faith in Jesus Christ, I hurt! And there is nothing I can do about it. Not now or ever.

Jesus wept.
(John 11:35)

Weep with those who weep.
(Rom. 12:15)

seven

Shall I tell you what has helped me the most through my grief? People of compassion!

The messages, the cards, the calls, words of encouragement, expressions of sympathy all have helped. Some more than others. But the people who really penetrated to my inner self in this time of raging sorrow were those who looked deep into my eyes, who hugged and sometimes kissed me, but whose look even apart from words communicated empathy and compassion.

I sensed that their spirits were crying. Sometimes the tears would trickle from their eyes. Not everyone is capable of communicating at such a depth, but those men and women who possess that rare quality touched my inner self.

It's not that they say much of anything. Sometimes they say nothing. Their eyes, their touch, their tears communicate enough. And that is so healing.

Do you remember the day you and I went to visit our friend Jim at his electronics laboratory? He showed us a laser beam. How that beam shot out in a clean, single light and penetrated the surface! That's how the compassion of these feeling people touched me. Like a laser beam reaching deep within and healing my unutterable hurt.

The people who empathized the most are parents. Not all parents, of course, but some special parents who hold a tender love for their own children. They need not necessarily have lost a child of their own to project concern. But, if they have experienced what I'm experiencing they show a special tenderness. Come to think of it, though, there are some people who are not parents, some not even married, who also have reached me.

I guess it doesn't depend on the state you're in, married or not, but on who you are.

Jesus wept over the death of a friend.

The ones who love the most, feel anguish the most. The more absorbing their care, the more profound their hurt. The most loving people are the most compassionate people. That is how true comfort has come across to me.

Do I then pain so much because I love you so much? Perhaps. But I'm not about to stop loving others because I've lost you. No, in fact I'm determined to love even more, to care more, to make the most of every relationship every day.

However angry your hearts, do not do wrong;
though you lie abed resentful, do not break silence:
pay your due of sacrifice, and trust in the Lord.

Know that the Lord has shown me his
marvellous love;
the Lord hears when I call to him.
(Ps. 4:4,5,3, NEB)

eight

I'

d like to share some other things that are happening down here since you have been taken from us.

Your friend Jeremy helped me clean out your room. It took us several days! You rigged up so many electronic projects and some of those we had to dismantle. And you know how much stuff there was to clean out! After your room came the attic where you had piled boxes of parts, old TV sets, Halloween stuff—because you always put on a terrific show in front of our house on that night—and all kinds of electric gadgets.

Jeremy just works away at it. He doesn't say much. He never did talk a lot. But he feels the sorrow, and I can tell that he's really hurting on the inside.

Sometimes he comes over just to sit and talk awhile. I'm giving him anything of yours that he wants; I'm sure that you would want him to have whatever he can use. I also gave him your bike. He never had one of his own, you know, and he's so proud of that 10-speed.

Both Mitch and Randy wanted one of your black and

white television sets, and I gave them one each. They're old but they still have good pictures.

Remember how you wanted me to buy a new TV set? You really thought our 10-year-old one showed a fuzzy, bleached picture and you were so eager for us to get a new one. You would have bought it yourself if you had the money. Well, we sold enough of your electronics equipment and old sets, and put enough money together for a new set. So you really bought us that new TV, and every time we look at it for the next 10 years we will think of you!

You bought Sharon her horse. Yes, you did. She sold it, remember, just before you were shot. She wanted so much to keep that horse. So I bought the horse back out of your savings and paid off all her debts. You couldn't have done anything better for your sister! Now every time she rides Buddy she'll thank you and remember.

You did so much for your friends. After attending your funeral, they've been walking up and down the street with a little more seriousness. When they walk by our property they remember you. The street isn't as raucous as it used to be. In fact, less than a week after the fellows carried your body to the cemetery, they drove over to see the grave. Randy told me (can't you just hear him?): "We're going to have a little talk with old Dave. We're going to the cemetery and see our buddy. He'll be there, talking with us."

I waited, waited for the Lord,
he bent down to me and heard my cry.
He brought me up out of the muddy pit,
out of the mire and the clay;
he set my feet on a rock
and gave me a firm footing;
and on my lips he put a new song,
a song of praise to our God.
Many when they see will be filled with awe
and will learn to trust in the Lord:
happy is the man
who makes the Lord his trust.
(Ps. 40:1–4, NEB)

nine

Y ou touched so many people through your sudden death. We received many expressions of faith. Let me tell you about three of them.

A mother who was locked in a continuous battle with her son, evaded changing their relationship. She could not overcome her annoyance and anger at him. Following your funeral she wrote that she realized she wouldn't get a second, third or fourth chance. "There are no guarantees on his longevity just because I have problems and request a time extension."

She didn't think she could handle the guilt and bitterness if a death occurred in her family, and she added: "Life is precious, vastly more than I normally allowed myself to believe." She is making some attempts to change herself.

A young woman had married for keeps. But even though they were both very strong Christian people, their marriage ended up in divorce. A couple of years later she remarried, but she was still plagued by doubts about the loss of that Christian marriage with so much promise. Why had God allowed it to turn out so

37

miserably? What was the purpose of that period of failure? She wrote:

"Your sharing at David's funeral was a very special testimony of faith. I'm sure everyone there was encouraged, as was I to know that in spite of your tremendous loss, you can still trust that God is working it all together for good. I don't understand what happened and I hurt deeply for you all. But if you can believe that God allowed this to happen for a reason and that He is a loving God, then, so can I. The funeral gave me a sense of victory, not defeat, and I'm sure that David would have liked that."

And then there was a mother in her thirties who six months earlier had buried her husband, the father of her young children. Suddenly and without warning he died. She started to attend church and she accepted Christ as her Saviour. In spite of her faith, she found much difficulty accepting the love of God. Here is what she wrote:

"Today I saw what God can do. Your strength was a testimony to Him. What I can say now, finally, is that six months ago I asked the Lord to come and dwell with me. Every time I 'got down' I prayed for strength and courage. For all that time though, I doubted His love. Until today. I have never been able to accept John's death as God's will. How much grief I could have saved myself if I could have. The example you set for me today was so comforting. Finally, today, I accept God's will. I know He loves me and I know that He hears my prayers, for He has answered them."

If these three lives were the only ones you touched it would have been enough. But I have a feeling that you're going to affect many more.

Who knoweth not in all these
that the hand of the Lord hath wrought this?
In whose hand is the soul of every living thing,
and the breath of all mankind.

Behold, he breaketh down,
and it cannot be built again:
he shutteth up a man, and there can be no opening.
Behold, he withholdeth the waters, and they dry up:
also he sendeth them out,
and they overturn the earth.
With him is strength and wisdom:
the deceived and the deceiver are his.
(Job 12:9,10,14–16, KJV)

ten

The words Job spoke during his great trial have been quoted to me by some believing Christians. *The Lord gave and the Lord has taken away. Blessed be the name of the Lord* (Job 1:21).

That is a comfort to me, and I echo Job's faith. To be assured that God has been in this, that He has taken you back to Himself, that He gave you to us in the first place if only for a little while, is consoling. Nevertheless another thought plagues me.

Maybe *the Lord* gave you to us, yes, but it was *man* who took you away. What did God have to do with the firing of that gun? Anything? Isn't this the way the world actually operates? Isn't this what takes place all the time? Is God in control? If God is in control, why does He allow evil men to shoot innocent young people? Or why does He allow all sorts of injustices and inexplainable calamities? What answer is there to such questions?

I have long ago answered those questions for myself, and that makes it easier for me somehow. They are not the burning, pressing concerns, because I have separated in my own mind what God does and what man is allowed to do in freedom. People are free to build and destroy, to make peace or war, to love and hate. That is why a crazy man can point a gun and shoot you down. God is not responsible. It's not what God wants. Absolutely not!

But then God didn't want the wickedness in the world in the first place. God didn't want human sinfulness. God didn't want war or death or misery. How could He? We chose our own misery in freedom and rebellion. Yet we don't want all that hatred and killing either. If, then, imperfect humanity doesn't want murder, how could perfect Love desire your untimely homicide? No, that doesn't fit together.

Nevertheless, God allowed it to happen. So I would like to rewrite the words of Job: *The Lord gave and man has taken away. Blessed be the name of the Lord.* A man was the instrument. In spite of man's evil, the last phrase stands sure! His name is blessed forever. Only mankind is evil. God is good.

You know that I've always believed that God is perfect. God is love. The Creator is not to be challenged or questioned or accused by His creation. But in an evil world evil men take matters into their own hands and play God. They kill innocents like you. (It happened to so many in Bethlehem when Jesus was born!) And that is not easy to forgive or accept.

But I don't think we have another choice. I don't blame God, but I blame that man. I don't judge God but I think that man deserves to be judged justly.

In case you think that I've gone too far in rewriting Job, I have another Scripture that makes the same point. The death of Jesus was foreordained and yet Peter, in

Acts 2:23, accused certain individuals of carrying out the sentence. Human instruments were responsible for the shedding of blood on the cross, even though it was allowed by the will of God.

And there will be a judgment, unless they (and we) bow to receive the free pardon that is given us by the grace of God.

If the foundations be destroyed,
what can the righteous do?

The Lord trieth the righteous:
but the wicked and him
that loveth violence his soul hateth.
Upon the wicked he shall rain snares,
fire and brimstone, and an horrible tempest:
this shall be the portion of their cup.
For the righteous Lord loveth righteousness;
his countenance doth behold the upright.
(Ps. 11:3,5–7, KJV)

eleven

Contemplating justice, I've come to another con-
clusion. I've always believed that God is a loving God
and that He is the Judge of the world, but it has been
difficult for me to harmonize those two in my mind.

Now, since your sudden death, it's coming into focus
for me. It's like those two images you see when you sit in
the ophthalmologist's chair. He asks you to line up the
two into one, and he stops moving them when you see
them as one. That is what happened to me for the first
time as justice and love blended together.

I understood how a loving God can allow His Son to
die on the cross, and yet remain the Judge of the world. I
have always leaned to the side of love and minimized
judgment, probably because I would rather be loved
than judged. Now there has arisen within me a sense of
justice, of righting the wrongs that exist in the world.
Mainly because you, you of all people, became an
innocent victim. I truly believe it is *right* to bring that
man to justice. He dared to shoot you down for no
reason at all, and he killed you.

I now grasp why the God who loves to the uttermost

45

and offers His unconditional pardon to all who believe is also the Judge of the universe. Those who refuse to accept that love place themselves outside of that love. Those who refuse to accept their responsibility for the death of Jesus leave themselves wide open for the coming judgment.

There can be no other way. Just as a man guilty of murder cannot be dismissed as if the crime is of no consequence, so mankind, guilty of the murder of the only begotten Son of God, cannot be dismissed without a just judgment.

And yet God will pardon all of us offenders for all of our offenses, when we repent and believe. That is the beauty and truth of the gospel. We are no longer under condemnation. We are given our unconditional release through faith in Jesus Christ.

As I begin to line up justice with mercy, judgment with love, in my mind, I'm discovering even more difficulty with the words Jesus spoke from the cross: *Father forgive them; for they do not know what they are doing* (Luke 23:34).

How could He pray like that? How could He ask forgiveness for His murderers? There is more depth in the love of Christ than I have ever seen before! Could I forgive your killer and his accomplice? That seems too much to ask, at least at this point in time. I expect justice, and yet, if your murderer or his accomplice would accept Christ as Lord and Saviour and repent, I know that I will also forgive them. I have no other choice. If Christ can receive them, so must I.

I need to add another thought. Although I want the state to prosecute and seek justice, nothing will bring you back again.

That means that even justice is empty. Locking that man behind bars will offer no relief to my pain. Nothing in all the world can bring you back. Nothing can make you live again.

Of course I believe in the resurrection of the body. Of course I know that you will rise from the dead. So will we all. But we live in the now, and that "now" is empty and lonely. It hurts because of you, David, because of the person you are, and the relationship we enjoyed that was so special to both of us. It really was very special.

I cannot reminisce in the past nor dream about the future. I can only realign the meaning of my life with the God and Father of our Lord Jesus Christ. I sincerely want to do that, although I'm often distracted.

If a tree is cut down,
there is hope that it will sprout again
and fresh shoots will not fail.
Though its roots grow old in the earth,
and its stump is dying in the ground,
if it scents water it may break into bud
and make new growth like a young plant.
But a man dies, and he disappears;
man comes to his end, and where is he?

If a man dies, can he live again?

I know that my redeemer liveth,
and that he shall stand at the latter day
upon the earth:
And though after my skin worms destroy this body,
yet in my flesh shall I see God.
(Job 14:7–10,12, NEB; 19:25,26, KJV)

twelve

I have mixed emotions about seeing you lying there in the casket for the last time. On the one hand I'm glad we had that special hour for the family, just to be with your body, dressed up in some of your good clothes. And Mother placed in the casket your Bible that you were given when you were six, and Sharon gave her puka beads, the kind you always liked.

On the other hand it wasn't you. It didn't look like you, really. You were cold and unsmiling. It was no way to remember you, but then it was better than nothing. As I say I have mixed feelings, for some people hold onto those last moments and others prefer to remember the living as they were.

When the police drove me to the hospital just after you had been shot, they advised me not to see you. And I didn't.

So it was right for us to come to you in that quiet room, because we had decided to close the casket for the funeral. Of course there were some tears, but most of us held up well. I'm glad your mother displayed her bright

49

and beautiful faith. She was an inspiration to many. Even though Grandma and Grandpa were fighting their tears, they managed very well too. You know how much they loved you. You were their only grandson. As Grandpa left the room for the last time, he turned once more to you and waved his arm and said, "Good-bye." It was very touching.

It's difficult remembering you so cold and hard and buried in that casket. But it's also grievous to recall you right here, racing through the house after slamming the screen door, and opening the refrigerator with your hands all full of grease and grime from working on your electronics. You didn't want to take time to wash your hands before getting the pizza out and sticking it into the oven. That's because you wanted to live so much, to continue your fun and enjoyment at top speed.

And I remember you in the evening bursting in to make popcorn in your special popper, heating the butter on the stove, and pouring yourself a glass of lemonade. And then with your hands full of popcorn, drink and ice, heading back out to your room. That was just about the top for you. You could eat popcorn every night, or was it peanut butter and jelly smeared real thick on graham crackers?

You loved to spice up your life in the same way you poured salt and pepper over your food like crazy, or let your oatmeal swim in heaping spoonfuls of brown sugar. You spread those bologna sandwiches with so much mustard that a jar would hardly last a week. Everything to the extreme, everything the most, that's how you lived. That's what I remember.

And that memory causes me special sorrow. I know how much you enjoyed life, how you could hardly stop to take a breath. You wanted to drain life to the very last drop. Well, you did. You lived everything to the hilt. I guess only that bullet could have stopped you cold in your tracks.

It wasn't fair, David! You didn't have a chance. And that's what throbs in my mind, like an artery continuously pumping fresh memories feverishly, fervently, and piercing. It was so unfair!

We are looking all the time not at the visible things but at the invisible. The visible things are transitory: it is the invisible things that are really permanent.

We know . . . that if our earthly dwelling were taken down, like a tent, we have a permanent house in Heaven, made, not by man, but by God.

We have to live by trusting Him without seeing Him.
(2 Cor. 4:18; 5:1,7, Phillips)

thirteen

Yesterday I stood by your grave. The earth was still fresh. Only recently was your casket covered, the grass laid back into place and a vase sunk just about over your chest.

I stood there a long time. It was as if I couldn't move. I thought of you six feet under the soil. This is not the place where you should be. This is not the time of your life when I should be driving to a cemetery and standing over your grave. Again I resented the man who put you there. It isn't fair or just or right.

I'm not angry with God. I accept what has happened. You know and God knows that my faith is not in question. It's like a story Jesus told about a wedding. Five of the 10 girls had prepared for the coming of the bridegroom by buying extra oil for their lamps. As they were ready when he came, so I have prepared for life's crises. The Lord has supplied the oil. Even as I'm using it now the supply is being replenished. I'm not afraid of emptying that supply.

But neither all my preparation for life's crises, nor

53

anything I can do now will bring you back. You're down there, or to be more correct, your body is down there and that's not right. Of all the wrongs in this world the one horrendous wrong that concerns me now, standing by your freshly dug grave, makes me powerless to change anything! There's nothing I can do.

I've always helped you. You know how many times I've rallied to your side. I stuck up for you whenever I felt you were right. That got me into trouble at times, but I couldn't stand it for you to be taken advantage of or wrongly accused or unfairly punished. And when, during these last few months, you borrowed money and couldn't return it, I kept on paying your debts, because one of these days you were going to turn that about. I believe you would have, because you wanted to.

Remember, just a few weeks ago, when you accidentally broke a picture tube on a color set you were repairing? The only time you had an accident like that. So who had to replace it? That was OK, David, it was only a hundred dollars. And now I'd give any amount to get you back.

That helpless feeling makes me furious. And frustrated.

If I didn't believe that your spirit is with Jesus, that you're alive and well, it would be unbearable, because it's hard standing by that grave and realizing that it's all over. All over for this life.

I will need to concentrate more on life than on death, on your perfection than our imperfection, on the vastness of eternity rather than this limited time.

My thoughts today are resentful,
for God's hand is heavy on me in my trouble.
If only I knew how to find him.
(Job 23:2,3, NEB)

fourteen

You're probably aware, David, that I've been talking quite a bit about justice. I feel that very personally. But I need to repeat it to myself: Justice won't bring you back, and therefore it's not all that important!

It's true, of course, that without a trial your death would seem to hold little value. That a man can just shoot you down, if he so chooses, and go free is more than I can stomach. Not just for my sake, but yours.

In all this concern for justice, my mind has been racing back to the greatest injustice this world has ever witnessed—the murder of the one and only Son of God. Jesus of Nazareth was fair, innocent, righteous, loving, honest, truthful, Godlike—everything a man should be. He was perfect, and yet they murdered Him. Surely that was most foul, unjust, unfair and criminal.

But God Almighty, the Father of our Lord Jesus, allowed that crucifixion to take place! And from that perspective I've attempted to view the problem of suffering in the world. There is so much suffering! Terrible wrongs continue to take place. Yet suffering does not diminish the compassion of God; not one iota. If the perfect Son of God was killed when He was sent here for our good, then why should we question unfairness when it happens over and over again?

Why should I be preoccupied with the problem of injustice when it strikes? Possibly because a just God has given us the sense of right and wrong. If we simply ignore the evil, we diminish our sensitivity and our caring.

Pondering the greatest injustice of all at the cross of Jesus has eased my sorrow.

Is that not the purpose of the cross? Is that not the meaning behind our calling God the *God of all comfort?* Isn't this the way by which He *comforts us in all our affliction* (2 Cor. 1:3,4)? I am allowing the truth that *the sufferings of Christ are ours in abundance* (2 Cor. 1:5) to reinforce me.

And yet, God rules in righteousness and truth. We can expect His justice. The world will not get off for the murder of Jesus. Only those who repent, believe and live out their faith will be allowed to enter the Kingdom of God.

Thank God, the Father of our Lord Jesus Christ,
that He is our Father and the Source of all mercy
and comfort. For He gives us comfort in our trials
so that we in turn may be able to give the same
sort of strong sympathy to others in theirs. Indeed,
experience shows that the more we share Christ's
suffering the more we are able to give of His
encouragement. This means that if we experience
trouble we can pass on to you comfort
and spiritual help.
(2 Cor. 1:3-6, Phillips)

fifteen

Two letters arrived today from families who had each buried a child—a 15-year-old boy like you and a little 5-year-old girl. Both because of illness. The circumstances were somewhat different, but the feelings are similar.

Both parents wrote that time will heal but the hurt will always remain. God will comfort us, but a certain ache and emptiness will never vanish. I think I know what they mean.

They spoke of God's comfort, and yet I read undertones of personal anguish that made them sensitive and kept them in touch with the sorrows of others. Indeed, their tenderness brought comfort to me as I walk through the valley of the shadow of death.

One sentence left a lasting impression:

"It has been nearly 11 years since our precious Kristi Ann went home to be with the Lord (or was it yesterday? or 100 years ago?) and only one thing is sure—God is sufficient for every need that we have."

I believe that. This mother has experienced it—for 11 years. But it seems like a hundred!

I know I need to lean more on God's grace.

I want to become more sensitive to the hurts and needs of others. I want to share the comfort with which I have been comforted.

I'm glad that those who have lost a son or daughter admit that the loss will always persist. We will never forget. The wound may heal, but the scar is a continual reminder of what once was and can never be again.

It helps to know that we are not alone in our grief. It is quietly healing. Especially when I consider that your mother and your sister are walking through the same valley that causes my pain, I tend to be less introspective. And we can walk together! Our mutual sorrow requires mutual perseverance.

It was right and proper that in bringing many sons to glory, God (from Whom and by Whom everything exists) should make the Leader of their salvation a Perfect Leader through the fact that He suffered.

He . . . became a human being, so that by going through death as a man He might destroy him who had the power of death, that is, the devil; and might also set free those who lived their whole lives a prey to the fear of death.
(Heb. 2:10,14,15, Phillips)

sixteen

Browsing through the New Testament I stumbled across a bold statement. *Death . . . belongs to you* (1 Cor. 3:22). Paul affirms to us that everything belongs to us, and he includes death. As if we need no longer fear. As if it's alright for us Christians. In fact he adds later in that same letter those famous words: *Death is swallowed up in victory . . . O death, where is your sting?* (1 Cor. 15:54,55).

What I need to recover is the right understanding of death which I had before your murder. Why has that all but shattered because of the firing of one bullet? I saw death defeated by the risen Jesus. I saw death surrounded by love and vanquished by the victory of Christ. That is why Paul could affirm that death belongs to us.

David, if I can again realize that death is surrounded by love, I will not resent your removal from our midst. Then I will not be tempted to believe that all the love we poured into you was lost. Love is never lost! It does not look for returns. It is not measured out with the expectations of reward. Love is unselfish and gives merely to enrich.

I want to continue to believe that, so that I can catch a glimmer of light from the essence of love.

Of course the memories of love throb with pain. A painting of many colors would hardly be a work of art if it contained only one hue. In life, as in art, many feelings mix together. And we can't escape the admixture of feelings, nor do we want to.

The memory of the dead gives life its more serious side, but I don't want to become overly serious. Walking around with a long face all the time is hardly the Christian way. Love adds bright colors.

There was always something so fine about you, David. You wanted people to be happy. You were concerned whenever you saw me unhappy. You told me not to be upset, and I can still hear you saying: "I don't want you to be unhappy, Dad! Don't be upset."

So I need to remember that Jesus has conquered death, that He has promised life to all who believe, and that the first Christians did not meet the grim reaper at Jesus' tomb, but angels.

Death belongs to me . . .

You have been "ransomed" . . . by the costly
shedding of blood. The price was in fact the
life-blood of Christ, the unblemished and
unstained Lamb of Sacrifice. . . .
God chose Him to fulfil this part before
the world was founded. . . . And God raised Him from
the dead and gave Him unimaginable splendour,
so that all your faith and hope might
be centered in God.
(1 Pet. 1:18–21, Phillips)

seventeen

I never told you about the one story in the Bible that always gave me the chills. The fact is, I had never told anyone my reaction, not until the day of the funeral. I stood in awe of the story, and every time I read it I choked up on the inside.

The story concerns Abraham, the father of faith. He was a great man of faith. Remember him? We read about him at family devotions a long time ago. He was promised a son, but he had to wait for the fulfillment of that promise for 25 years! (We waited for you 13 years before you were brought into our home.)

When Isaac was born, he became the delight of his father. Abraham loved him more than anyone or anything, this child of promise. Through Isaac, Abraham's seed would become like the stars in the sky for multitude.

But one day when Isaac was about 14 years of age, God demanded the supreme sacrifice of His servant Abraham. He told him to take his only son up on a mountain and offer him to God.

I do not for the life of me understand why Abraham obeyed. Nor how he could obey! The Bible states that he showed tremendous faith, but what a test that must have been for him. To take his only son, lay him upon an altar hastily built on top of the mountain, bind him with cords, pull out a knife and proceed to kill him right on the spot. Only the voice of God stopped him at the crucial moment, before he was able to plunge the knife into Isaac's body.

How could Abraham proceed that far? I never could have done it. I often told God that I would do anything He asked, anything at all, as long as He wouldn't ask me to offer my only son. I could not bear to lose you. That is the one thing I could never accept or do.

And now I have had to yield. I could never approach the faith of Abraham; now I've been urged to step into his shoes.

No heavenly voice stopped that speeding bullet from penetrating your flesh. God allowed you to be taken. He may have had His own reasons, but He allowed it in His providential will. Things turned out a little different from the Abraham story, for Abraham sacrificed a ram in place of his son, and he was able to embrace Isaac when he untied him from the altar. What an embrace that must have been, with tears and tugging of heart!

I'm not allowed such an embrace. Mine was not the Abraham story; mine was the crucifixion story.

If it must be so, then so be it.

I can honestly echo the words of Job: *Shall we indeed accept good from God and not accept adversity?* (Job 2:10).

I will not charge God foolishly. After all, He is the

eternal God who offered His only Son for us on a cross. He did not stay His own hand! He did not substitute a ram. He offered up Jesus for us all.

And if that is the God who has made us and re-deemed us, He will be with us in our supreme test of faith. In Him I put my trust.

[Jesus] Himself endured a cross and thought nothing of its shame because of the joy He had in doing His Father's Will; and He is now seated at the right hand of God's throne.
(Heb. 12:2, Phillips)

eighteen

O ver my typewriter hangs a replica of a Dali painting of the crucifixion. You've seen it there, David. You used to talk to me about it. Remember how I explained it to you one day? You listened, very intent.

It's the only painting of the cross of Jesus I have seen that does not show Jesus' face. The view is from above. We look down on His shoulders and His bowed head. The cross is suspended in midair. At the foot of the cross, clouds, colored by the morning sun, float. The sun remains hidden behind the horizon, and clouds hover over a fishing boat in the foreground of the crystal blue lake of Galilee.

That suspended cross, which is elongated as it reaches down toward the world below, holds up Jesus, hanging high above the world, His muscular body outlined against a pitch black background. That setting reveals the very darkest black you have ever seen, while a spotlight falls as it were on the shoulders of our Lord. Since the view is from above, the thick darkness enveloping the cross speaks to me of the suffering of the Father—God's suffering at the death of His only Son.

Dali's painting signifies to me that God Himself is touched with the most excruciating pain anyone of us is asked to endure. God Himself experienced the agony of suffering, the affliction of torment, the cruelty of murder. God Himself became helpless, unable to demonstrate His power or His love by saving His Son from torturous death. He could have done something. He could have done everything! But He chose to do nothing.

He remained helpless for our sake. For the salvation of the world.

God experienced that loss, that death, that killing. And being a father, David, I am comforted by this truth. Our heavenly Father has suffered so utterly, so completely and so willingly.

He understands! To know that the eternal God understands and cares is so healing, so consoling. And that, after all, is the thrust of all the Scriptures that recount the deeds of salvation from the Exodus to the Crucifixion.

I am not alone in my agony. He *is* with me.

O that the grounds for my resentment
might be weighed,
and my misfortunes set with them on the scales!
For they would outweigh the sands of the sea:
what wonder if my words are wild?
The arrows of the Almighty find their mark in me,
and their poison soaks into my spirit.
(Job 6:2–4, NEB)

Yea, though I walk through the valley of the
shadow of death,
I will fear no evil: for thou art with me;
thy rod and thy staff they comfort me.
(Ps. 23:4, KJV)

nineteen

I don't quite know how to tell you what it's like handling grief. Words are difficult.

When I'm alone I don't want to remain alone. When I'm with people I become restless and want to retreat into my shell.

Conversations often contain such trifles. Friends mean well. They attempt to cheer me up by keeping things light, but a heavy seriousness runs through every day. A little like the notes of Beethoven's Fifth Symphony, repeated over and over again, so that you cannot tear them from your mind. That recurring score almost rips the inner self apart.

When I'm alone, I'm restless with concerns that provide no answers. God is real, but God is not always present. Truth remains truth, but all the verses of Scripture stay upon the page and refuse to leap into my heart. I do not doubt the truth or wisdom of God, but neither do I feel His everlasting arms about me.

Perhaps that is because I've never experienced that kind of Christianity. Not so much feeling but more faith, God asked of me.

I marvel as I recall that even Jesus cried out on the cross at the time of His greatest need: *My God, My God, why hast Thou forsaken Me?* (Matt. 27:46). He believed in the presence of God but experienced His absence!

We don't want it to be like that. That's the hardest thing to accept. It isn't supposed to be like that either. We have all those promises in the Bible that God will never leave us or forsake us. And He does *not* leave us; only, where is the certainty, the assurance? More often there is only dumb recognition that we're on our own.

And yet I believe that I'm not on my own. It only seems as if God has somehow left me, left me to walk all alone through the valley. Even as I write this thought, I know the certainty which sounds from the Twenty-third Psalm. He walks through the valley with me. It's just that I don't feel Him; but then I'm not supposed to walk by feeling. Only by faith.

Perhaps my loneliness is accentuated because of the void you've created. The old times will never return, the fun times and the good times we used to have are gone forever. We can't go back into the past. Nor will the future repeat the past. No matter how much we may want it to. Life is moving into something new and different.

In some ways I don't want the new, simply because you won't be a part of the new. It's like moving out of the house where you lived with us. I don't want to move. I don't want to leave you behind as if to say: "We're going now. I don't care anymore."

I can *never* say that.

One day we may have to move, but not yet.

My tears have been my food day and night. . . .

O my God, my soul is in despair within me. . . .

Deep calls to deep at the sound of Thy waterfalls;
All Thy breakers and Thy waves have rolled over me.

Why are you in despair, O my soul?
And why have you become disturbed within me?
Hope in God, for I shall yet praise Him,
The help of my countenance, and my God.
(Ps. 42:3,6,7,11)

twenty

I've questioned why words of comfort fail to comfort me, even from Scripture. The Bible is supposed to help us, but why are there times when those words fail?

The people of the world do not have our Christian faith. They mourn the dead without hope. Some fear the consequences of the next world, some believe that we must first pay for our sins before we can be at peace, and others state categorically that death ends it all. As a Christian I am told that I need *not grieve, as do the rest who have no hope* (1 Thess. 4:13). Why am I not consoled by that verse?

Even the most encouraging quotations often leave me flat.

I found one answer by reading C.S. Lewis. He recorded his feelings when he lost his beloved wife. He wrote that only those are comforted by the Bible who love God better than the dead!

This provided me with an insight into your mother's faith. She indeed holds onto the Scriptures fervently.

She experiences great comfort. She loves God most of all and often speaks of her love, her faith and respect. Whereas, to tell the truth, I probably still feel the conflict of loving you too much. I'm not able to rest quietly on the promises of the Bible.

It's the old conflict I was sharing with you from the Abraham story. I told you I couldn't understand how Abraham chose God above Isaac. But that was what Abraham did, even to the point of death.

You see, I do want to glorify God and enjoy Him forever. Still it's tough to write off all my fatherly concern, all the compassion, all those hopes I held out for you. Now you will be unable to continue our family name (and you were the only son in our family who could have done so)! You will be unable to receive the joys of living, to father your own son and daughter, to reach your potential, to live life to the full.

I'm very sorry about that. It makes me sad.

Yes, I believe you are in a better world and you have a better life than we do here. It sounds most comforting, but even that peaceful truth cannot erase all those natural hopes I had for you.

Surely our griefs He Himself bore,
and our sorrows He carried.
(Isa. 53:4)

twenty-one

Some people want me to forget my grief. They distract my mind.

On the one hand I realize how dangerous it is to nurse one's sorrows, but I must have my quiet moments. I don't want to ruminate in my poignant unhappiness. I need to feel that friends understand, that they sorrow with me, even if they don't.

The apostle Paul encourages us in our faith that we sorrow not as others, but he also says that we are to *weep with those who weep* (Rom. 12:15). This is healing in itself—when you realize that someone else feels and understands and allows you the freedom to overcome your special loss.

On the other hand life must go on. Sometimes I don't want it to. I want to retain a special minute of silence that is often observed at public gatherings in memory of some celebrity. I just need those private minutes to do honor to your memory so you will not fade away into oblivion.

For who will remember? The memories are almost

sacred. The moments of quiet too few. The music plays ceaselessly in the background and the voices of people drone on about so much trivia.

I feel life hurrying by, passing over the dead and crying out, "It's over with and gone; it's all in the past. Don't become a martyr!" And I consider that cry almost irreverent and unacceptable.

Sometimes, you see, I just want to scream. To scream as loud as possible! A scream wants to emerge from way inside of me, from my gut. But how can it bring you back?

What good will it do? Is a scream like a releasing of all those tensions within? Or is it a way to let the world know that something is terribly wrong? Someone has wronged you and I cannot right the wrong.

I'm tired of being calm all the time, super controlled, on top of every situation.

To be in touch with my feelings is to give vent to the *indignity* of it all. That's why I am tempted to scream at the top of my voice.

I find some solace in the fact that Jesus screamed from the cross—*Why hast Thou forsaken Me?* (Matt. 27:46). Perhaps that groaning, piercing yell expressed His inner turmoil. Perhaps that scream relieved His pent-up tensions too.

Suddenly I understand (probably understand it only slightly) why Jesus shouted at the top of His voice in the agony of His suffering. And I'm glad He did. He was very human, completely human.

He knows what I feel! Jesus is no stranger to the depths of my sorrow. He has, in fact, gone beyond my agony and pain.

This is the God with whom we have to do. This is our

Saviour and our Lord: identifying with us, warm, human, comforting, caring, loving—*a man of sorrows, and acquainted with grief* . . . *Our griefs He Himself bore, and our sorrows He carried* (Isa. 53:3,4).

Where now, O Death, is your power to hurt us?
Where now, O Grave, is the victory you hoped to
win? It is sin which gives death its power,
and it is the Law which gives sin its strength.
All thanks to God, then, Who gives us the victory
through our Lord Jesus Christ; for He has delivered
us from the fear of death, the power of sin and
the condemnation of the Law!
(1 Cor. 15:55–57, Phillips)

twenty-two

You know, David, I can't bring these thoughts to an end. I should conclude my conversations, but I have a feeling that they will continue for a long time to come.

What I want you to know now is that in your short life you brought so much to so many people in so few years. And I want to thank you especially for what you have given to me.

You taught me about fatherhood. You, more than anyone else. Because of you I have come to understand the fatherhood of God. I couldn't even begin to tell you what I have learned about love and compassion, tender feelings and even discipline, about the many-sided revelations of the heavenly Father.

You've helped me to like children. Before we had children of our own we kind of liked children, but after you came we *really* liked them. You made such a change.

Your sensitivity reached me. I perceived behind the shell of your roughness a quiet spirit that longed for love and peace. When you deserved some form of discipline, or you knew that I had become angry because you went too far, you would ask for forgiveness and you always meant it. You may have turned around again the next moment and repeated the same wrong, but as you grew you really wanted more than anything to be accepted, to keep peace, to have everything go right. And I'm glad that was always true of you.

The best gift you gave me was yourself! Perhaps the crowning moment came last Father's Day, one month before you were killed. With the little money you had— and it was very little because you incurred many debts— you bought me a card and a bumper sticker. You wrote personal messages on the card. That would have been enough, but the sticker really got to me.

I told you that very afternoon that I never put bumper stickers on my car. Not even Christian ones. The reason is mainly because I don't like to advertise myself. But even though your sticker called attention to me, I couldn't help but keep it right on my bumper. It read: "You're following #1."

Thank you, David. How could I ever forget you? You said it all when you gave me that present. That's why I told you that you're a very special person. And that's why I want you to know that your life has not been lived in vain.

After all, it's not quantity but quality that counts. The greatest life ever lived was abruptly cut off after 33 years.

Thanks, David, for everything. I don't want to let you go, but I have no choice. I believe you're in good hands. I trust those nail-pierced hands.

And someday when I too step out of time into the circle of eternity, please come to welcome me!

And I saw a new heaven and a new earth; for the
first heaven and the first earth passed away,
and there is no longer any sea. . . . And I heard
a loud voice from the throne, saying . . . "He shall
wipe away every tear from their eyes;
and there shall no longer be any death;
there shall no longer be any mourning, or crying,
or pain; the first things have passed away."
And He who sits on the throne said, "Behold, I
am making all things new."
(Rev. 21:1–5)

Dear David,

This is a kind of P.S. Some months have elapsed since I wrote the earlier experiences of my grief. Today is the six-month anniversary of the day you were shot.

Did you know that every month I've made a note of the twenty-second? Today, looking back over the landscape of the past and rereading my reflections on your sudden death, I want to add some more impressions.

With the passing of time we heal. The cycle of life returns. Any desire for retribution also fades. The wound of unfairness heals over by the mercy of God. Now in those moments when I experience a sharp jab of sorrow it's because of the loss, the emptiness, the reality of death.

I recently read this statement and pondered its wisdom: "Life isn't necessarily fair. But it doesn't have to be fair to be beautiful."

We pass through various stages in our grief. At first there is a dull denial of death, as if it couldn't have happened. You were so much alive one minute and then

93

you were gone so completely and so brutally. It seemed impossible to believe and accept. It couldn't be true.

The stage of denial soon passes into hot anger. I experienced a demand for justice, I lashed out against all injustice. I knew those hurt feelings were not right, but they were real nevertheless. They could not change the fact of death and they left me feeling so completely helpless. Such anger can become dangerous. During that period we are capable of doing something irrational which we would later regret.

From that seething hurt and anger it is possible to slide into the stage of depression. Being of a strong nature, I attempted to avoid both severe depression and dumb resignation, although I must admit there were times when life lost its glow; when there wasn't much meaning left; when some feelings of despondency punched their way through the protective layers of my faith.

But then comes the dawning of acceptance—the final and best stage when one can accept things as they are. I can go on in faith. My life moves ahead. This is not to say that there will not be times when I again feel that brutal stab of pain, like the poke of a needle in my flesh.

You see, David, we not only remembered the date of your death monthly, but we also celebrated your sixteenth birthday. That was hard for us. We brought home a pizza because you enjoyed pizza like crazy. We reminisced. Later that evening your cat which always slept on your bed curled up in my lap. She does that often, and I sometimes wonder if she misses you. If only she could talk! She always reminds me of the way you used to hold and pet her.

And then Christmas came. We gathered with the

94

family and missed you terribly. We didn't talk about it much. Maybe it was too painful. And now it's the twenty-second—six months later.

There will be other memorable days. I don't look forward to July 22 this year or the next or the next. Of course I feel anguish. But there is an acceptance now of both the anguish and the abundance of life, an acceptance of the hurt but also the hope we have in Christ. The agony of death and the assurance of resurrection.

So faith renews and reshapes our lives.

Let me share some final thoughts on this poignant day.

God is big enough to absorb our anger, our hurt, our pain. He is not destroyed by our feelings, nor by death itself. God is not only faithful but wonderful, allowing us to pass through those various stages, being there all the time, and finally healing us with His love. That which is beyond human power to repair is not beyond God's power to renew.

Death is not static. It is not a state of sleep. It is not the end. Your grave, real as it is, is not the only place for me to look. You are with God. Death leads to fulfillment, to growth, to the experience of the new, to the joys described in the book of the Revelation.

I recall a saying of D.T. Niles: "We live as those who are dying. We die as those who are living." At the end of life's hall hangs that black curtain, and eventually we must pass through it. But we die to live eternally, to be with God. The certainty of that truth becomes more real as time passes.

The end of birth is death. The end of death is birth. And that birth leads to new life!

Jesus is both on this side and the other side of that curtain. He is both here and there. For Him death holds no boundary since He is our risen Lord. He is with us to the end here, and He is with you there. And that is forever true! You already *see His face* (Rev. 22:4).

God is the *God of all comfort* (2 Cor. 1:3).

I'm underlining the *all*.